D0117016

Cursive Writing

Around the World in 26 Letters

PRACTICE WORKBOOK

FlashKids

ISBN 978-1-4114-6345-5

Distributed in Canada by Sterling Publishing
c/o Canadian Manda Group, 165 Dufferin Street
Toronto, Ontario, Canada M6K 3H6
Distributed in the United Kingdom by GMC Distribution Services
Castle Place, 166 High Street, Lewes, East Sussex, England BN7 1XU
Distributed in Australia by Capricorn Link (Australia) Pty. Ltd.
P.O. Box 704, Windsor, NSW 2756, Australia

For information about custom editions, special sales, and premium and corporate purchases, please contact Sterling Special Sales at 800-805-5489 or specialsales@sterlingpublishing.com.

Printed in Canada
Lot #:
2 4 6 8 10 9 7 5 3
03/14

www.flashkids.com

Even in the age of computers and hand-held devices, handwriting is an essential skill. Help your young learner master this beautiful art with *Cursive Writing: Around the World in 26 Letters*. In addition to teaching the form of each upper- and lowercase letter, this book introduces the landmarks in and around 26 fascinating cities. Lush, postcard-quality artwork illustrates the unique charm of each location.

TO SUPPLEMENT THE HANDWRITING AND GEOGRAPHY SKILLS YOUR CHILD LEARNS IN THIS BOOK, CONSIDER THE FOLLOWING ACTIVITIES:

- Have your child write, in cursive, a page-long report on a location of interest.
- Ask your child to handwrite a letter to a friend or relative. Remember to have him or her hand-address the envelope in cursive.
- Challenge your child to draw a travel poster for one of the locations in this book. Make sure all the writing on the poster is in cursive!
- Encourage your child to handwrite a paragraph or two about what makes your city or town special.

Aa

a a a a a a

a a a a a

a

a

Athens Athene

airplane

avenue

address

A is for Athens

A is for Andrew + by

Dad

a A

a a

A A

a a

Athens

Athens

a a a a

The Parthenon >

Athens is in Greece.

Now write your own sentences.

NO WAY!

In the 600s BCE, some laws in Athens were very harsh.

Stealing bread or fruit was punishable by death!

B b

B b

b b

B

b

Beijing

boat

beach

bridge

B is for Beijing

B B

b b

B B

b b

Beijing

The Temple of Heaven >

Beijing is in China.

Now write your own sentences.

NO WAY!

The Great Wall of China runs across northern China. It is about 5,500 miles long, 15–30 feet wide, and 16–26 feet tall. It is so big that it can be seen from space!

C C C C

c c

C

c

Copenhagen

compass

continent

culture

C is for Copenhagen

C C

c c

C C

c c

Copenhagen

< Temple of Tivoli Gardens

Copenhagen is in Denmark.

Now write your own sentences.

NO WAY!

As one of the world's first amusement parks, Copenhagen's Tivoli Gardens has what many believe to be the oldest Ferris wheel and roller coaster still in use today!

Dd *DD*
dd

D

d

Dublin

desert

delta

domestic

D is for Dublin.

D D

d d

D D

d d

Dublin

< Dublin Castle

Dublin is in
Ireland.

Now write your own sentences.

NO WAY!

The name "Dublin" comes from the Irish words *dubh linn*, which means "black pool." The Dubh Linn was a lake where the Vikings anchored their trading ships in the mid- to late 800s!

E e

E E

e e

E

e

Edinburgh

east

earth

equator

E is for Edinburgh.

E E

l l

E E

l l

Edinburgh

Royal Yacht Britannia

Edinburgh is in Scotland.

Now write your own sentences.

NO WAY!

Edinburgh Castle is the site of much of Scotland's political and military history. But it is also home to a dog cemetery! Soldiers' dogs have been buried there since the 1840s.

$\mathcal{F}f$ $\mathcal{F}\mathcal{F}$

ff

$\mathcal{F}$

f

Freetown

flag

forest

folklore

F is for Freetown.

F F

f f

F F

f f

Freetown

< Cotton Tree at the City Center

Freetown is in

Sierra Leone.

Now write your own sentences.

NO WAY!

The first settlers of Freetown were freed American slaves in 1792.
They built their settlement around a cotton tree that still stands today!

Gg

Gg

gg

Gg

g

Guatemala City

gulf

globe

geography

G is for Guatemala City

G G

g g

G G

G G

Guatemala City

< Pacaya Volcano

Guatemala City is in Guatemala.

Now write your own sentences.

NO WAY!

Guatemala has over 30 volcanoes! Only three are active today. Over 84,000 years ago, one of the volcanoes exploded and collapsed, forming Central America's deepest lake, Lake Atitlán.

H h

H H

h h

H

h

Helsinki

hotel

harbor

history

H is for Helsinki.

H H

h h

H H

h h

Helsinki

< Uspenski Cathedral

Helsinki is in
Finland.

Now write your own sentences.

NO WAY!

November through January in Helsinki is very dark. Because it is so far north,
the city only gets six hours of sunlight a day during the winter!

Li i Li I

i ii

I

i

Islamabad

island

import

industry

I is for Islamabad.

I I

i i

I I

i i

Islamabad

< National Monument of Pakistan

Islamabad is in Pakistan.

Now write your own sentences.

NO WAY!
Islamabad is home to one of the largest mosques, or Islamic temples, in the world.
Construction of the Faisal Mosque took a decade to complete!

$\mathcal{J}$ j $\mathcal{J}$ $\mathcal{J}$
j j
$\mathcal{J}$

j

Jerusalem

jet

jungle

journey

J is for Jerusalem.

J J

j j

J J

j j

Jerusalem

< Damascus Gate

Jerusalem is in Israel.

Now write your own sentences.

NO WAY!

Running underneath part of the Old City of Jerusalem is Zedekiah's Cave. It is a 5-acre limestone quarry—the source of the stones for Solomon's temple—that was carved over a period of several thousand years. Legend has it that the quarry was also a secret escape route for King Zedekiah!

K k

Kathmandu

kayak

kinsfolk

knapsack

K is for
Kathmandu.

K K

k k

K K

k k

Kathmandu

Himalaya Mountains >

Kathmandu is in Nepal.

Now write your own sentences.

NO WAY!
Kathmandu sits amid the Himalaya Mountains. One of the Himalayas, Mount Everest, is the tallest mountain in the world. It keeps getting taller each year!

Ll

L L L
ll

L
l

Lima

landmark

longitude

language

L is for Lima

L L

l l

L L

l l

Lima

< Plaza Mayor

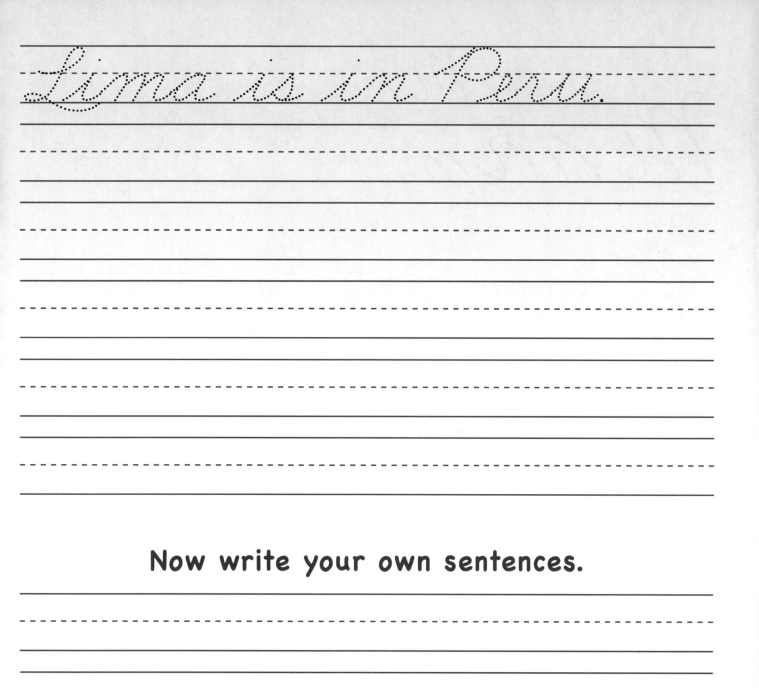

Lima is in Peru.

Now write your own sentences.

NO WAY!

Lima is just outside the Andes Mountains, where the potato originated.

Over 4,000 varieties of potatoes come from the Andes!

M m m m m

m

m

Manila

map

museum

monument

M is for Manila.

M M

m m

M M

m m

Manila

Manila is in the Philippines.

Now write your own sentences.

NO WAY!

The country of the Philippines is an archipelago, which is a group of islands.

It is made up of 7,107 islands in all!

$\mathcal{N}$ n n n n

n

n

Nairobi

north

nation

neighborhood

N is for Nairobi.

N n

m m

N n

m m

Nairobi

< Animal Sanctuary

Nairobi is in Kenya.

Now write your own sentences.

NO WAY!

Nairobi has many animal sanctuaries where visitors can see lots of animals up close, including rhinos, lions, leopards, cheetahs, hyenas, buffaloes, zebras, and wildebeests. You can even feed tall giraffes!

O o *O O*

o o

O

o

Ottawa

ocean

origin

overseas

O is for Ottawa.

O O

o o

O O

o o

Ottawa

< Parliament Building

Ottawa is in Canada.

Now write your own sentences.

NO WAY!

The Rideau Canal is a waterway that runs through Ottawa. In winter, the canal freezes and part of it is used for skating, making it the world's largest ice skating rink at almost 5 miles long!

P *p* *P* *p* *P* *p*

P

p

Prague

park

peninsula

population

P is for Prague.

P P

p p

P P

P P

Prague

< Prague Castle Guard

Prague is in the Czech Republic.

Now write your own sentences.

NO WAY!

The word *robot* comes from the Czech Republic! It was first used in a Czech play called *Rossum's Universal Robots*, written by Karel Čapek.

Qq

Q q

q q

Q

q

Quito

quake

quarry

quarter

Q is for Quito.

Q Q

q q
Q Q

q q
Quito

Mitad del Mundo >

Quito is in Ecuador.

Now write your own sentences.

NO WAY!

Ecuador is named after the equator. The imaginary line passes right
through the country just north of its capital, Quito!

R r *R r*

R

r

R

r

Rome

ruins

river

region

R is for Rome

R *R*

r *r*

R *R*

r *r*

Rome

< Trevi Fountain

Rome is in Italy.

Now write your own sentences.

NO WAY!
In ancient Rome, people used a very unusual ingredient to whiten their teeth.
They cleaned their teeth with human urine!

Ss

S s

s s

S

s

San Juan

south

sightsee

skyscraper

S is for San Juan.

S S

s s

S S

s s

San Juan

El Morro >

San Juan is in
Puerto Rico.

Now write your own sentences.

NO WAY!

A little frog called the coquí is the unofficial mascot of Puerto Rico. Unlike most frogs, the coquí is not born as a tadpole—it is born as a tiny frog!

T t

T T T

t t t

T

t

Tokyo

train

travel

tourist

T is for Tokyo.

T T

t t

T T

t t

Tokyo

< Tokyo Subway

Tokyo is in Japan.

Now write your own sentences.

NO WAY!

Tokyo is one of the world's most crowded cities. In fact, at some of the busiest train stops, workers called *oshiya*, or pushers, are hired to cram as many people into the train cars as possible!

U u

U U

u u

U

u

Ulaanbaatar

urban

upland

underpass

U is for

Ulaanbaatar.

$\mathcal{U} \mathcal{U}$

$\mathcal{u} \mathcal{u}$

$\mathcal{U} \mathcal{U}$

$\mathcal{u} \mathcal{u}$

Ulaanbaatar

< Statue of Damdiny Sukhbaatar

Ulaanbaatar is in Mongolia.

Now write your own sentences.

NO WAY!

Like many of the country's inhabitants, the capital of Mongolia, Ulaanbaatar, is a nomad! The city changed locations more than 20 times before settling in its current location in 1778.

V v

V V
v v

V

v

Vienna

visit

valley

village

V is for Vienna.

$\mathcal{V}$ $\mathcal{V}$

v v

$\mathcal{V}$ $\mathcal{V}$

v v

$Vienna$

< Schönbrunn Palace

Vienna is in

Austria.

Now write your own sentences.

NO WAY!

PEZ candy was invented in Vienna, Austria, in 1927! It was originally
a breath mint—PEZ comes from the German word for peppermint, *pfefferminz*.

W w

W W

w w

W

w

Washington, DC

west

world

waterfall

W is for
Washington, DC

$\mathcal{W}$ $\mathcal{W}$

w w

$\mathcal{W}$ $\mathcal{W}$

w w

Washington, DC

< Washington Monument

Washington, DC is in the United States.

Now write your own sentences.

NO WAY!

The White House in Washington, DC, is considered by some to be one of the most haunted houses in America. There have been many stories of encounters with ghosts of former presidents, first ladies, and even a cat!

X x x

X Xx

x xx

X

x

Xalapa

x-axis

xotic

xperience

X is for Xalapa.

X X

x x

X X

x x

Xalapa

Olmec Head >

Xalapa is in Mexico

Now write your own sentences.

NO WAY!

Jalapeño peppers originated in the city of Xalapa, which is sometimes spelled Jalapa.

Because of this, the natives often refer to themselves as Jalapeños, or "hot stuff!"

Y y

Y y

y y

y

y

Yucatan

y-axis

yacht

yonder

Y is for Yerevan.

Y Y

y y

y y

y y

Yerevan

Yerevan is in

Armenia.

Now write your own sentences.

NO WAY!

A candy factory in Yerevan broke a record and created the world's largest

chocolate bar in 2010. The bar weighed 9,702 pounds—that's heavier than a female elephant!

Z z Z z Z z

z

z

Zagreb

goo

gone

zephyr

Z is for Zagreb.

Zz Zz

Zz Zz

Zz Zz

Zagreb

< St. Mark's Church

Zagreb is in Croatia.

Now write your own sentences.

NO WAY!

Kuna, the Croatian currency, was named after a rodent! In medieval times, the pelts of this rodent (known in English as the marten) were traded in place of an organized money system.

Practice the letters.

Aa   Bb   Cc

Dd   Ee   Ff

Gg   Hh   Ii

Jj   Kk   Ll

Mm   Nn   Oo

Pp   Qq   Rr

Ss   Tt   Uu

Vv   Ww   Xx

Yy   Zz

Finish each sentence.

I live in

_____

- -

_____

I would like to visit

_____

- -

_____

because

_____

- -

_____

- -

_____

Draw where you live.

Write the name of the city and country pictured.

Writing Time!

Write about your favorite place you have visited. When did you go?
Who did you go with? What did you see while you were there?
Would you want to live there? Why or why not?